KITCHEN HYMNS

Also by Pádraig Ó Tuama

POETRY

44 Poems on Being with Each Other: A Poetry Unbound *Anthology*
Feed the Beast
Poetry Unbound: 50 Poems to Open Your World
A Casual Kindness (in collaboration with Vox Liminis)
Sorry for Your Troubles
Readings from the Book of Exile

MEMOIR

In the Shelter: Finding a Home in the World

THEOLOGY

Being Here: Prayers for Curiosity, Justice and Love
Borders and Belonging: The Book of Ruth; A Story for Our Times (with Glenn Jordan)
Daily Prayer with the Corrymeela Community

KITCHEN HYMNS

PÁDRAIG Ó TUAMA

CHEERIO

First published in Great Britain in 2025
by CHEERIO Publishing
www.cheeriopublishing.com
info@cheeriopublishing.com

10 9 8 7 6 5 4 3 2 1

Typeset in Perpetua by Martha Sprackland
for CHEERIO Publishing.

Printed and bound by TJ Books Ltd.

A CIP catalogue record for this book is available
from the British Library.

ISBN: 978 1 73944 057 2

For Heather Walton, Sam Tongue, Pat Bennett and Greg Fromholz.

In sweet, living and loving memory of Glenn Jordan and Daniel Fry.

Ordo Missæ

KITCHEN HYMNS

DO YOU BELIEVE IN GOD?

KITCHEN HYMNS

IN A GARDEN BY A GATE

KITCHEN HYMNS

Dieu a tout fait de rien.
Mais le rien perce.

God made everything from nothing.
But the nothing persists.

Paul Valéry

KITCHEN HYMNS

Jesus . . . both faith and magic have failed

Patricia Smith

In The Name of the Bee

I asked the grasses if they believed
but they said *believe* is a poor verb.
I asked the sun but it had eclipsed.
I asked the tree, and it said stand.
I asked the fieldmouse, it nibbled
a seed in my outstretched hand.
I asked the hare, but it didn't stop. I asked
the ground but it just kept spinning.
Things grew, then died, then rotted, then
renewed the soil. New things grew. I went to ask
the bee about the future but it had gone
extinct with a bead of nectar on its tongue.
I asked the songthrush about the soul
and it sang until a gate to hell opened.
I asked the mountain what mattered.
It said nothing.

Mother Brendan's Opening Words at Ash Wednesday Mass

Darlings, look around.
Next to you's the nurse, the cleaner, the doctor, the child-
minder, the waiting, the hoping, the barely surviving,
the can't-get-out-of-bed-can't-sleep-can't-cope.
There's the teacher out of work, the disaffected
priest, the taxi driver, the shopkeeper, broke shareholder,
tourists, retirees, waitresses, bankers, administrators,
the tired and committed, the excited and the stressed.

I know you expect me to bless you in the mysteries of God,
but I prefer the strangeness of each other, darlings.
Look around.

In the name of whatever
reason brings you here. In the name of anything
that works. In the name of nothing.

Are you burning yet? You will be.
Take this cup and drown your sorrows.
Take this bread and butter it. Lick it.
Taste the salt. Nothing made you come here.
Nothing stops you going.

The Long-Tailed Tit

He picks fleece from wire,
fluff from dryers, bog cotton, moss
and hair. Silk from webs, flax
from spiders' eggs, packs it all with lichen.
She plucks feathers from the corpses
of the wren, the siskin,
blue tit, coal tit, goldcrest.
Adds her own feathers too.

She takes tickets, tissues, scraps
from the pockets of passersby.
That child who dropped a ribbon
will never find it.

Thousands of these things,
carried in a tiny beak,
or clutch of claws. It takes weeks.
They take turns keeping watch
on their soft sock of bricolage,
camouflaged at the fork.

They work in pairs, hawking
the walls smooth with their long tails
to keep their dull eggs safe.
They'll stay two weeks, or three.
Uncles feed the chicks
when the parents are away.
They stay warm in winter
huddled in a volary of brown and pink.
Then in spring, call out to one another

as they move from tree to tree.
Tsee-tsee, they sing, tsee-tsee.

Eat This Bread

The way you hold your mouth open
and you hop after your mother,
wanting food right from her mouth.

The way you ask and ask and ask
as if you know you'll die if you don't.

The way you swallow, then open up
your mouth again. You don't know
what satisfaction is. The way you
tantrum your wings. You ball of air and
emptiness. Your cheeps are
me me me.

You are unceasing. A baby. A bomb.
You are all hunger, no flight or song.

The way the light shines through the
tissue of your beak. Your eyes wide.
Round. The raw need, the pink demand
of you. I can't stand you.

Do You Believe in God?

I don't believe in God, I said, and she said Oh?
Somehow I thought you'd managed to keep that going
even though I haven't. She asked if I'd told others.

Yes, I said, I have. I mean, it's not like I'm
saying I Know About What Is. It's just that the burden
of belief isn't on me anymore. God, it feels much freer.

I believe I'm in the room next to belief. I hear
the sounds of prayers coming through the walls. I like
the smell of incense. And the sound of fabric rustling fabric

as the people stand or kneel. Sometimes I can tell
the text by the intonation of the reader. I mutter
the responses underneath my breath. Lift up your hearts.

And do you? she asked, Lift up your heart?
Yes, I said, I do, but I don't know to who.
Whom, she said. Let's get started on the soup.

DO YOU BELIEVE IN GOD?

Gelobt seist du, Niemand.

Blessèd art thou, No One.

Paul Celan

Do You Believe in God?

My grandad came from Abbeydorney, near Tralee,
and so the Banna Strand was always in his memory.
When we – my dad, his dad, and me – visited
my great-uncle, they discussed the land, and family,
debts due to drink, and neighbours.
I threw myself from dunes, believing I could fly.
I climbed up to the top and arched my back against its peak,
seeing only blue. The long drive home
was famine roads, laid by starving men
whose grandchildren my grandad knew.

Do You Believe in God?

My dad went fishing at the Old Head cliffs.
Mackerel by the dozen – cast out, reel in –
placed fresh dead meat
inside a stripy plastic bag.

When he saw the wave,
and knew that it was big enough to take him,
he threw his things away –
his penknife and his favourite rod,
the bag half-filled with gutted fish,
the hooks, their small feathers.

He lay face down on jagged rocks,
and felt the sea attempt to take him to the sea.
It scraped his skin away. He held on, prayed
that the wave would not consume him.

Do You Believe in God?

Every summer, crowds of them, down from Belfast, Lisburn,
Holywood and Larne. *Mission groups*
they called themselves, *Going down to Ireland.*

Their work was the sharing of the Gospel.
Local Protestants would host them in spare rooms,
have barbecues and singalongs, catch up on the Northern news.

They'd meet for prayers, then they'd go bear witness
in our village, bringing tracts in plastic envelopes.
Do you believe in God? they'd say to people.

The Irish accent's sometimes hard to understand, one said
to me on Carrigaline's Main Street.
Not you. You're easy. How good that Pastor introduced us.

He likes you. He said you've been Asking Questions.
I wanted friends and language and a purpose to my future.
But mostly friends. They told me I was *On the Way.*

The priest passed by one day, coming back from the Vigil Mass.
Do you believe in God? the missionary asked.
The priest seemed amused by their enthusiasm for the Lord,

but looked at me with curiosity. *Tell your father I said hi*, he said.
Classmates saw the version of me I wanted them to see.
Never Miss an Opportunity, one missionary told me,

sharing chips and ketchup after worship songs and testimony
on the village green. A handsome boy from school
was chatting to the Northern girl with curly hair.

He's been through a lot, she told us, later on that evening,
and is still confused by grief since his daddy died last Easter.
We huddled. Someone prayed for his salvation.

Impromptu, they sang 'Lord I Lift Your Name on High'
while waiting for the bus into Cork City. Locals noticed them
and noticed me. *You're Ann's son, aren't you?* someone said.

Are these lovely singers practising for a concert? In the town
they discussed strategy and success with the other teams.
They invited me to join them. I had nowhere else to be.

He's got a Roman Catholic Background, I overheard one say,
discussing me. I repeated Roman to myself, I repeated Background.
Do you believe in Mass? a missionary asked.

The question seemed like asking me if I believed in toast, or tea,
or beatings. Plain facts. *Are you asking if I like it?* I asked.
He doesn't understand, she said, looking straight through me.

When they were gone, the streets were like they'd been
before. Lonely. Known. I walked the long way home from Mass
hoping for a greeting from anyone I recognised. The tide was in,

I skimmed stones along the estuary, listened to the mocking ducks
and watched the disappearing sun. I remembered
what they said about salvation as they drove away.

Do You Believe in God?

It'll hurt he said   I said *I know*

You're sure? he said   I'm sure

His weight on me
pushing into me

placing himself in me   Making me
with   Agony   and

Please
It was abandonment and
Yes   And No   And
More   And more
manly
than I'd thought   anything
could   be

It was   Take
Everything   that I'd been begging   to
experience

It was Sweet

Fury

It was
deliverance

Do You Believe in God?

Before it became my blood,
my muscle, fat and shit,
I masticated it with spit.
Before that, it was in heat
– I used juice to make it rise –
and before that, it was wheat and milk,
soda, oats, salt and seeds,
unpacked from bags, car home, basket, shop
and truck, factory and farm.
It was whatever makes up life,
rot, manure, and us.
I cut and butter it, swallow it,
lick my lips, want more.

Do You Believe in God?

It used to be the hare and not the rabbit
that was the harbinger of Easter.

They'd know all about new life –
born with both eyes open,

alone within hours of their arrival,
learning how to feed while frightened,

nocturnal, sheltering in forms, fucking each other
in the morning, eating bark, eating shit,

running because life depends on it, knowing
how to kick and kill a fox, speed of the underworld

with ears pinned back, dropped hips, eyes fixed
on survival, hinges in the skull to absorb the shock.

Boxed? Box back. Feed your babies
once a day. Leave them.

Do You Believe in God?

At twenty-three I walked in the dark
to Bull Island's stretch of beach.
I stood beneath the statue of the
Virgin Mary. Star of the Sea.
I took off all my clothes and shouted
I am lonely at the water.

It was the middle of the night.
There was the smell of oil
and rotting seaweed,
the glow of factories,
smoke catching all the light
from Dublin city.

Do You Believe in God?

He heard a voice.
    What are you doing, Pádraig?
Is this the voice of God? he asked.

The voice said *Find*, then *God*,
    then *Nothing*. It went dark. He found a chapel,
lit a candle. Nothing struck him.

He felt old fractures, tried to integrate. But
    he failed. Disintegrated. He left, got lost. He went exploring,
thinking only of escape and pleasure. He could not believe

what he was planning. He went looking
    for a man. When he found him, he watched the man undress, say
something with his eyes, say Yes.

They faced each other naked. He was afraid,
    aroused, alive, amazed. Nothing interfered. Nothing spoke
as they both got busy biting nipples, licking

armpits, busy tasting salt and musk
    from cracks, busy turning over and turning a man over,
busy using stubble as a tease. Busy being held

against a wall. Busy being taken.
    Busy taking back. Busy with a body
not a question.

Do You Believe in God?

I accepted it for far too long,
lay down, said Yes, said Anything you want,
said I'll follow.

I took that path, learned all the rules.
I was told I was a natural.
I begged graces from a you.

It ended.
With a word. What word?
I don't remember.

Some voice said, Here's a map, drive off it.
When do I come back? I asked.
You don't, it said.

Here's a road, a sleeping bag, a stove, a bit to eat, it said,
and a night of stars, a fox along the border, a buzzard in the sky.
A hare whose speed you'll need.

Here's more grief. And sorrow. And a book. And
a number for a friend.
Leave tomorrow.

I tried anything
I could get my hands on.
I dreamt of different endings.

I paused instead of searching for the way.
I found nothing and nothing
never felt so good.

I return sometimes. Sometimes I like it.
I like the smells, the psalms, the bells for prayer
at midday and at six,

the feeling of the beads between my fingers,
the touch of skin to lips when someone
puts a story in my mouth.

Do You Believe in God?

I turn to you,
not because I trust you,
or believe in you,
but because I need a direction for my need. You –
the space between me and death; you –
the hum at the heart of an atom; you –
nothing; you – my favourite emptiness; you –
what I turned away from and will turn to; you –
my ache made manifest in address; you,
silent you, what my friends saw as they died; you
contain what's not containable; you –
shape of my desire –

Do You Believe in God?

It was like arriving home from school
and not finding disarray – relief,
today at least. It was like growing too big
to be beaten, like that woman who hugged you once,
and the memory rekindled instead of sleep.
It was like fingering the stitches,
like thinking there was time, like stories at a wake,
like kissing the body goodbye.
It was like a storm and like its eye. Like winning
just one fight. Like pressing that sweet bruise.
It was like tonguing the gap
where the tooth was

Do You Believe in God?

Though I've lost God, God is
the only language that I speak.
I need to describe this loss.

I thought he appeared
and disappeared. Now God's
nowhere, though this loss

is like memory carried in a gust
of air, a scent. I make myself
describe what I have lost

with attention to the yearning
I still have. But I fear
God became a word

to bear all I could not bear.
God bore it well. No
containing now. An empty shell.

I have a need, or grief,
for what was never there.
I have lost God. God
is the only language that I speak.

Do You Believe in God?

The last thing I did was sweep the floor.
I'd washed the sheets, made the bed,
thrown things out, given things away, given more.
I left the bathrooms gleaming, put down seeds for birds,
and watched hares through the kitchen window.
I saw a young one hop across the patio, I hope it survived
the fox. The night before, with all the lights turned off,
I'd walked, with a lit candle, through every room,
remembering who and who and who and who
had been where. When. I said thanks to emptiness.
That last morning, I woke at three and heard the owl.
I went out naked, faced the field in the early light
and let the cold creep up my skin. I went back in,
and dressed, and listened. That's when I swept the floor,
and when I locked the door, and when I left.

KITCHEN HYMNS

A Mhicín mhúirneach,
Tá do bhéal
's do shróinín gearrtha,
Óchón agus óchón-ó!

Lament of the Three Marys

My darling son,
your mouth
and your small nose split open,
Alas, and alas-o!

Caoineadh na dTrí Mhuire

PB2G

Sure lookit, says I, here's the thing –

I love your writing, even though you're a homosexual. While it's not for me, I suppose the Lord reminds us that there's sin in everyone, and the sin in me's no less than the sin in you. Not that I ever partook, honest to God, I think I'd die of the mortification. Anyway, that's not why I'm writing to you. I'm writing to you because I couldn't get you out of my mind and I said to himself that I couldn't stop thinking of you, so he says to me, write the man a letter, it might do him good, and I hadn't thought of it like that before, so here we are and there's the ticket. Your book had me in tears half the time, the other half I didn't understand, but that's because I'm no good at poems, the nuns told us poems were full of notions, and whatever else I don't have, it's notions I have least of all. You wouldn't do me a favour would you, would you send me a copy of your book with your signature? The address is on the back of the envelope. It would do me the world of good. Your own prayers made me want to get down on my knees with gratitude, and you a homosexual. Listen, I said to himself, this fella's one of them and yet he writes like that. God almighty, I thought, is it losing my marbles I am? But the Lord said if a branch bears fruit then a branch bears fruit. PB2G, I says, Praise Be to God, because I'd been terrible worried he'd disapprove. I've a fierce devotion to Our Lady, the BVM himself calls her, but I don't always hold with abbreviations. If a thing is worth taking time to say it's worth taking time to say. Woman, he says, would you hurry up, but I says no, a rosary told on old beads is as well told slow. He'd be through the sorrowfuls, joyfuls and the gloriouses in the time twould take me to say a single mystery, but each to their own I suppose. Better a fast prayer than no prayer at all. The woman down the road have a husband that wouldn't even open his mouth for a yawn in Mass, never mind a prayer. Not even the responsorial psalm. But your prayers, Joseph tonight, they got me through some tough nights, I can tell you that, ha? I hope now you're not septic with yourself, because nothing comes from you that comes from you, it's the Lord himself working through you. I brought a book of your prayers to the priest and he looks at it and says that it's nice alright but maybe a bit Protestant, and I says, sure look at the fella's name, could you get anyone sounding more like one of us than that, and he says he'll take a look at it and all, so I left it in His hands. I'll leave him a small reminder when I drop in his dinner tomorrow. You're up the North now, aren't you? God you're fierce good. All that fighting. Jesus wept. I can't be having with politics now, but I'm glad there's peace. I hope they sort it out and I hope they get on with it. Make no fuss. There's too much fuss about some things. I was only saying to my other neighbour yesterday that things have gotten much better since her son moved away. Whingeing and complaining the whole time he was, sure it was almost the death of her, but then she applied to colleges for him, to give him a funt out the door, twas the making of him – she forged his signature on the CAO forms, I saw her do it with my own two eyes, and I looked at her and I thought there's

forgiveness for everything.

Confession

My son told me he googled
Am I having a breakdown?
the other day.

Why did you do that? I asked.
Because I'm in pain, he answered.

No, I said, why did you ask the computer?
Why didn't you come to me?

He said he knew I'd say that.

I said I'm glad he knew it.
He said he's not. I almost said
he was acting like a fool,
but I saw his face.

What did Google say, love? I asked.

The Long Table

the dead seemed more alive to me than the living
Marie Howe

Today I get up early because Mags said it's the best time of the day. She wore yellow trousers and oxblood boots and died when she was twenty. And Georgie told me to be thankful when I'm busy. Relish everything you're doing, she said to me that Saturday. Dead by Friday. So I make time, in demands, to remember. And when I read a book, I place my hand on it and honour Glenn who worshipped words and friendship. He packed three times love into half a life. And when I swear, I swear from my gut, breathing out the words like smoke, just like Cathal said I should. I saw his mother at his grave a few years ago. She smiled and said, You come here too. Not a question, just a statement. I say what I need to say because of Graham, faithful as foundations, and as hidden. And though I never met him I think about Ignatius every day, down by my prayer tree. Gerry said a lot can be achieved with precision and a bit of patience. He sang songs to rivers. I listen for his voice. Eugene cut logs into his nineties, and lit lovely lively fires; I light candles when I can. Dan made handmade gifts, so I do too. Bridget wrote a letter every day. I managed two last year. Brendan tried to mediate all things, singing kitchen hymns every morning no matter where he was. I hear his sweet humming as I pick up my guitar and strum.

The Last Supper

They smelt the food as soon as they came in,
taking off their shoes, putting on the slippers
Mother Brendan kept for guests.

The stew and bread were good as always.
They sprinkled salt and pepper,
passed the plate of cheese, shared knives,
poured red or white. Later there was
chocolate, whiskey, water and strong tea.

They stayed over, held each other
under handmade blankets. In the bedroom,
sprays of lavender on the mantel –
her old aid for sleep.

In the morning, looking out the window,
they saw the cliff was dangerously closer.

Will you move? they asked her. Somewhere safer?
Of course I won't, my loves, she said.

Charade

Let's play charades, children, Mother Brendan said,
you know the rules: no mouthing, no signing,
simply hold a concept in your person and let us pick up the vibe.

Dónal went first. He just stood up. He beamed.
He was delighted with himself. Ontology! the children squealed
and everyone clapped. Lovely way to start, Dónal, said Mother B.
Easy, but elegantly done.

So. Someone else. Make it tough.

Quietly, with no rush, Máiréad got up
and, without touching anything, moved the light about.
Faces shadowed and unshadowed. They saw things
they hadn't seen before. They wondered how they'd lived
before they knew what they now knew.
If that wasn't a representation of
Sartre's preference for a process of becoming
as a critique of a more static Heideggerian concept of being,
Brendan said, I don't know what was!
Comparative analysis, not just propositional –
bravo Máiréad. Good girl yourself.

Breffni walked into the middle of the room.
And one child, then another followed,
moved near him, stopped, motionless yet alert.
Were they waiting? praying? decaying?
Some looked hungry, others looked like prey.
Equiprimordality! the watching children sighed, enraptured.

Breffni, Mother said, philosophers
are reassembling their atoms just to shake your hand.

Rafi took the stage, looking burdened, headached, grey.
Life went pale on faces. The class, already quiet, went quieter.
No one made a sound. They approached the edge of nothing, feeling fear,
annihilation. Years collapsed. Then imperceptibly,
like the moment winter changes, something. A crocus.
The work of what a smile can do. The mind called back.
Bruises cured themselves. Psychoneuroimmunology.
Mother Brendan scanned around, saw excitement
and exhaustion. It was time to end.

She left them to their own devices for a while. Some read.
Some put their head down on their arms and slept.
But then someone murmured from their dream,
someone's face went pale, someone stared across the room.
One child drew a circle on a circle on a circle, couldn't stop.
Mother Brendan chewed her sleeve.
How much time had passed?
Then she noticed Fatima, sunk into her chair,
drawing everybody's energy to herself.
Fatima saw that she'd been caught, grinned, and dropped her hold.

Who taught you about the quantum unconscious?
Brendan said, but Fatima just smiled.
Children, time in the future
is visiting us today with experiences
of the past we have not yet unpacked.
You'll see. And you'll remember.
Now. Have you no homes to go to? Out you go!

IN A GARDEN BY A GATE

The only legend I have ever loved is
The story of a daughter lost in hell

Eavan Boland

a compromise was at last reached. Core should spend three months of the year in Hades's company, as Queen of Tartarus, with the title of Persephone, and the remaining nine in Demeter's.

Robert Graves

natus ex Maria Virgine,
passus sub Pontio Pilato,
crucifixus, mortuus, et sepultus,
descendit
ad infernos,
tertia die resurrexit
a mortuis

born of Mary a Virgin
suffered under Pontius Pilate
crucified, died and buried,
he descended
to the inferno,
on the third day, he rose
from death

Symbolum Apostolorum / Apostles' Creed, fifth century

all the way down to shadowy Tartarus,
the deepest chasm underneath the earth,
beyond the iron gates, beyond the threshold
of bronze, as far beneath the land of Hades
as heaven is from earth.

The Iliad. 8.16-20 (translated by Emily Wilson)

Once upon a time a young god was sent to hell. She'd been violated, then blamed for her violation, which is a curse of time. Another curse of time was placed on her: winters in the underworld, the rest of the year above. She was winter, she was spring. When she ascended, the world awoke. When she descended, it lamented. She left; she returned. One year. Fifty. Five hundred. Forever. Powerful and powerless she was.

A different time, a different god, a different violation. He went to hell as well. Nobody knows if he was there for a minute or a year. Nobody helped. He sang songs to pass the time. He stopped believing in what he used to believe in; himself included. He licked water from the walls to satisfy his thirst. He saw hares. They seemed to know where they were going. He followed.

He found what he hoped was a way out: a long tunnel. He dragged himself along. He heard someone ahead of him. He couldn't catch up. She didn't look back.

Eventually, he felt a breeze. There was the smell of rain in the air. He forgot time, but kept crawling. Then he saw a gate: small and heavy. The woman was standing on the other side of it, still facing away. He crawled out and into a garden in early morning light. He collapsed on the grass. The dew wet his lips where he lay.

I heard you behind me, she said, I wondered who you were.
          Why didn't you turn back? he asked.
It doesn't work like that, she said. How did you find the way?
          What way? he asked.
To the gate, she said. To the garden.

Why are your mercies new every morning? Do they leak away at night? To
where? In a place with no sunrise, I reckon with the empty. In a place with
no horizon   no up   no down   no over there   no back here   no map   no
landscape   no season   no time   I find   I'm lost.   No one   to turn to
for help   or company   no distractions   no interruptions. Once the panic
goes, I sing hellpsalms. Then the panic comes again.

The Gate to the Garden

She heard him, of course. She wondered
who he was, and where he came from. How.

She'd made the rules. She knew he could only do this
on his own. One glimpse back,

one hand, one turn would send him packing.
He was bleeding, she could smell the iron in the air.

She imagined he imagined it was nearly over.
It took her centuries, forgetting everything

at every turn. Thinking she was new
when she was anything but new. Nothing worked

to help her. She gave nothing now but curiosity.
She felt the final scratch of winter on her skin.

Man's Search for Meaning

Could you get me some water? he said.
She looked at him and said,
Who died and made you God?

He closed his eyes, said, I am thirsty.

And what am I to you, she replied,
some servant you can order?
I waited for you, but not on you. I dragged
you to the shade and kept you safe,
warded off the insects smelling out your
sweat and clots.
I covered your body with my clothes.
You get me some water.

He said, Where's the well?
There isn't one, she said.

Then is there a river? he said.
A mountain stream? Is there rain here?
Where are we?

A garden, she said.
A place I come to often.

Can I stay? he asked.
Nobody can stay, she said.

Let There Be Lights in the Vault of the Sky

Would you say you had a purpose to your life?
she asked.
Why do you ask? he said.

I've been watching you, she said. You don't seem at ease
with waiting, you're hasty.
Sometimes bored, anxious, angry even, rough.

I know you don't sleep so well.
Up twice or three times, off along the glade towards
the gate. Then back, an hour later, sweating.

What do you do while I'm away? he asked.

I watch the stars, she said. I like them.
They're like siblings to me.
I miss them when I'm underground.

Look at those, she said, pointing – Seven Sisters.
I knew them years ago. They were abducted too.
I went down, them up.

I'm not living how I'd choose
if I'd been free enough to choose. Nothing of my life
is what I thought my life would be.

There Is Time for Time

When people ask where you have been, what
do you say? he said.

I say I've been to hell and back, she said. And they say,
Christ, me too. Then they tell me about their pains.
And they expect me to be shocked, so they offer
reassurance, say not to worry, not to fret,
nothing that a burger and a bottle can't improve.
Sometimes they might ask if I'm okay
after everything they've shared with me. I smile and tell them
I'm okay. Then they feel okay. They change the subject.
They pick up their phones and carry on.

But you, he said, what do you say? What story do you
tell yourself about
                                        what happened?

You're new to this, she said. You'll tell it one way
to yourself today, then you'll find the story needs to change.
Some days that's fine. Sometimes you'll feel you're
back again, can't escape. Then spring.
Then summer, autumn, winter. Spring again.
Time's not a line.

Who Do You Say I Am?

Who do you say I am? he asked.

You are such a
narcissist, she said.

Did you know him? he said.
Am I like him?

Yes, she said. Like you
he believed in things worth dying for,
and he died alone. Echo was left empty.
Deaths like that
are meaningless. Sacrifice is not salvation.
Beauty fades, purpose too.
And certitude.

I believe you, he said.

I don't think you do, she said.

On the Nature of Forgetting

She'd seen his wounds. Who couldn't?
But she knew she shouldn't ask
until he'd settled down a bit.
So, she watched. Waited.
Saw him bend his knees while he was standing,
balancing on the front part of his feet,
tightening the muscles of his ass and thighs,
always scanning the horizon – planning his escape.
She looked at his bare back,
his gasping panicked chest,
his mangled ankles.

Who did this to you? she said at last.

I forget, he said.
Forget? Or won't remember? she asked.

Is there a difference? he said.

Yes, she said, I can see you need to talk.
So talk to me. If not me, anyone, anything –
the sky, the earth, a fucking tree.

Can't, he said. Don't want to either.

On good days I say, Look what I survived. Waking to a weight of hatred every morning. Managing a day or two, or, if not quite managing, getting through. If the heart is stardust then it knows that quantum is the basis of the real. Collision. Crash. I've been smashing up against the heart of Nothing all my life. I feel it reaching into me, threatening to undo me. I don't believe much in the future. And now's no comfort either. Still, I breathe. Like this. And this. And this. I try to look around, try to notice. I see the flow of water coming from a pilgrim's offering far above. I see wet pawprints where the hares passed through.

Being and Time

Where are you going, she said.
I don't know, he said, I just need to go.

You don't have to, she said,
there is another way of being here
in time. Some things just unfold.
Let me hold you.

He was shaking.

It's not like death, this little death,
she said, mouth against his ear.

After, he was quiet,
and he slept.

She thought he seemed
less distracted when he woke.
Sex is good for grieving,
she thought. Sleep's a balm.

I gave you my heart, but then you gave it back. Not casually. Carefully. I found it on the altar where you left it. It was light, the meat, dried out. I tried to reinsert it in my chest and make it beat. I made the rhythm with my fingers. Ba-doom. Ba-doom.

Do You Believe in God?

Do you believe in God, after all that you've been through? she asked.
I'm not sure, he said. Do you?

Not like I used to, she replied. I grew up thinking
God was light, then I went to where there was no light.

I used to think that God made all things new, but I've been
wandering a while now – nothing's new.

Everything's a lens through which
another everything can be viewed. That screws you up.

And releases you. I look at dawn now, and love the turning,
the way that morning is both dead and new. How about you?

I like walking alone at twilight, he said,
I like the in-between.

She held his gaze, asked, Is that your answer?
It's all I've got, he said.

For Such a Time as This

Your mother said your father was
a god, she said. Mine said that too,

and I see what your god does.
Abandons, tests and traps you.

Asks for more. And more. Then more
than anyone is capable of doing.

That is not divinity.
That is a weak imagination.

I'm beginning to agree, he said,
but I don't believe he'd change.

I'm talking about you, she said.

I was no fool, but I wanted to love the world. Of course I knew dragonflies are as brutal as they are beautiful, and I'd heard how baboons plans revenge with intelligence and cruelty. I've seen what tornadoes do, and emperors too. I know what it's like to suffocate, sweat blood, betray and be betrayed. I've hummed the melodies of warpipes. I've been let down. But I wanted to believe it was possible to love the terrible world, love being alive, know that threat isn't the only pursuit, that nightmares aren't inevitable, and that courage is available especially in the worst moment. I liked the unexpected. Until it happened. I wanted to believe something mattered.

The Greatest of These

Who do you respect the most, he asked,
after a day they'd spent apart.

I don't like that question, she replied.
Why? he said, feeling tired.

It's *the most*, she said.
Your categories make me think
I'd have hated knowing you before.

Okay, so who do you respect? he asked.

Much better, she said, looking at the sky.
Today I'd say my mother,
even though I'm always glad to leave her
when the winter comes.
Yesterday I'd have said her mother,
who knew a portion was enough,
never gave too much.

Looking at my family and friends
is like looking through a fire,
he said. I remember two or three
who stayed with me until the end.
Then I woke. And then I knew.
There was no end. Just more.

The School of Dreams

She woke because he was shouting.
Everything woke with him – the animals, the nearby trees,
the sky, it seemed. He kept screaming,
then went quiet.
She heard him say

not everything that's lost is lost / not everything / forgotten needs to be remembered / there is a fire / that burns enough for comfort / there is a book / that ends

The Book of Revelation

What's your love language? he asked.
Leaving, she replied.

No, no, he said. There's five:
words of affirmation, touch, and gifts,
the fourth is time, and, damn, I forget the fifth,
I know it rhymes with purpose.

Where do you get this shit? she said. Anyway,
all of them. And death. Hunger too. And things I don't have
the words for.

It doesn't work like that, he said. In the book
you answer fifty questions and get results
by turning to the end.

You and your certitudes, she said.

Come on, come on, he said, just play along. Which one's yours:
words, or touch, or time, or gifts, or –
service! yes, that's the fifth.

Did you love your kids? she said.
Of course I did, he said.
How? she said. With words, or touch, or time,
or gifts? Or piles of knickers, jocks and socks
left laundered on the landing?

Fine. You've made your point, he said.

If you want to know, mine is words of affirmation.
I bet you yours is time.

I made you into a god you / inadequate you / you container with no containment / you master of this hollow / I made you / the standard / by which I measured purpose / smeared your words on those I barely understood / happy with your prophet / you called me holy and beloved / sexless I wandered through the world / hard for the hardhearted things / I thought pleased you / now / in the wreck of me / I still breathe badly / and I fear the need in me / the head the eye the throat / the heart and belly / cock and hole / (I see it too / I can't say *my*) / I passed through death / I fail at life

Desire and Its Interpretation

Do you have hope? she asked. He snapped, In what?
In hope, she said. Come on – I know you understand me.

It's the one I miss the most, he said. I used to think it was a little radio,
tuned to the secrets of the universe. Then I thought, No, hope's a muscle.
Then, No, a song.

There's Hope and hopes, she said. Hope in meaning,
small hopes for a nice day.

I hope for nice days, he said.

When everything was ending, I said a prayer back to myself –
one I'd learned at school. I never felt so empty as when I realised
it was empty.

She looked. Said nothing. Felt the edge of him. Felt the fray.
Understood that he was asking her for help he couldn't bear.
She saw him struggle, saw him try. Then,

I remember something else, he said, like how your name means destruction.
What does that mean? Are you the end?

Does it feel like that? she asked.

Don't patronise me, he said. I can't trust anything, and I don't know
who you are, or what you're here for. I just know that everything
I've believed is nothing now. The god I said I followed plucked me
like a golden apple, let me rot in the corner of his garden. Look at me now.
Cold on whatever day this is. Hungry too. Tonight I'll drink water

from the mountain stream – it'll taste of heaven and sheep's piss.
And I wonder if it's worth the effort to continue.

Is it? she said, Worth the effort?

He made a noise like laughter, or a bark. Who's asking? he said.
I know you want to know what happened to me, why I'm bleeding.
How come you found me? Were you waiting? Am I entertainment?
Am I bait? If I talk will you explode? Are you a friend? Are you a bomb?

Depends on what you want, she said.

Teach Us How to Pray

What bird is that? he asked.
A songthrush, she replied.

How can you tell?

She repeats herself, she said,
becomes her own song's echo –
singing and repeating, then listening to herself
and singing back.

They gather at the gate in choruses
and charm what's underneath
with melodies and harmonies and trills.
I love them. They sound like spring to me.

For a long time, before I found the gate
I'd find my way by listening for their song,
and singing back.

Now I Am Going to Destroy the Earth

late one night he woke her
i can't describe what happened he said but i can show you

he jerked his head
a cliff face fell
trees snapped in half animals scrambled
scattered he opened up his mouth and screamed
land cracked collapsed
dark matter swallowed up the sound
then shot it back

she understood this language joined him
eyes on fire she made
anthrax flowers rise and burn the garden
and the gate
she screamed with pleasure
as she ripped the sky
from her came the sound of a
universe exploding sounds of
yes cries of again
againagain
time started
folding and unfolding

what do you do with rage he asked
as she lifted up a mountain slammed it flat

this she
answered

Whosoever Shall Deny Me, I Will Also Deny

And you? he said.
Who did this to you?

He said he didn't
have a choice, she said.

He said nature, or an arrow,
made him do it.

I reject such fatalism. I build fires
with that language.
I can't abide someone who can't
admit complicity or a failure.

That's why I'll not stay with you
much longer, she said,
though it upsets me.

I Saw the Earth, a Void; the Heavens Too, Abandoned

How do you think your father
tells your story? he asked.

I neither know nor care, she answered.
I don't know either, he said.

The danger is you care, though, she said,
and that's a torture on a torture.
Make no mistake – he knows.
Control's a shade of creativity.

I turn to death, she said,
face the nothing,
address the void
with longing and return.

I don't think I'd find that easy, he said.
What's necessary's rarely easy, she said.

Drink and Be Drunk with Love

When do you masturbate? she asked him.

What?

You heard me, she said. When?

When do you? he pushed back.

Early mornings, she said.
Something about low light and
the promise of a day. I wake and make myself
a cup of pleasure, fill myself
with that exquisite pain.
Brimmed up and overflowing,
discovering, delivering, scraped
with the blade of all forgetting.
Making and unmaking heat and
electricity. God, I love that
nipple-aching edge of greed and giving,
the hunger in the sex of me. I become
the prowler and the prey.
I make love by taking
my sweet time.

Your skin is shining, he said.
I know, came her reply.

In a Garden by a Gate

You had a nightmare again last night, she said. You were screaming.

I was?

You were. I did the thing that's worked before.
Let my hand rest heavy on your sternum.
It only took a minute. You calmed down.

Why were you awake? he said.

I was about to leave, she said.

Would you have said goodbye?

We don't need goodbyes, she replied.
Everything comes again.
Now that you've been here, you'll be here again.

But you stayed, he said. Why so?

You need to be the one to go, she said.

A Sword Shall Pierce Your Heart

What's your mother like? he asked.
Like? She laughed. She is an event. Like nothing
else. She is like the heat that makes the oil in trees
explode. She's like the blade that slices
marble, or tufts of grass that make the limestone crack.
She's like the stream that trickles down the hill
then splits the canyon. She is like the dew
that rots the grass. Why do you ask?

I was thinking about mine, he said. She spent her life
observing me. Giving me attention. Once
I saw her picking up the toenails I'd just cut.
What are you doing? I asked her. Never mind, she said,
they're mine now. She was a mystery
to me. Storing things inside her like an
arsenal for a war she never waged.

I like the sound of her, she said, and I bet
she's got pent-up rage. I would have,
if I'd had you to raise. You're not easy.
You'd have been a complicated son to mother.

There Is a Time for War

Most mornings they ate bread,
left the crumbs,
moved a bit away,
waited for the birds.

They loved one young finch.
Half-sized, fierce and hungry.
His green was the green of green.
They watched him beaking up the seeds
that had fallen from the crusts, fighting off his siblings,
spreading his small wings, flaring out his tail,
tufting up the tiny feathers on his head.

This is why I do not turn to you, I am terrified you'll answer. This is why I do not light my candles, I fear I'll see you. This is why I do not call to you, or seek you, cry out to you, or make my body a blank page for you – I think your words will come and crush me, bruise and break me. I close the book. I do not lift a pen. I postpone your mercy because I do not want your mercy. I remove your hand from mine. I write about the absence I have forced you into. I prefer your exile, like I like my exile. I nail your name in places I will never see again.

You Must Be Born Again & Again

When would you say your life began?
she asked.

When I found this garden, he said. And there you were,
watching me, back turned towards the gate.

Mine starts every year, she said.

Going up? Or going down?

You know me well by now, she said,
even though we're strangers.

That's called avoidance, he said.
That's a fair assessment, she replied. What will you do today?

I think I'll leave, he answered.

Just like that?

Just like that.

Do you know a way?

No, he said. I'll make it as I go.

you touched my mother with death / and stitched me / into your thigh for a while / there i grew / what you lacked in love / you made up with brutal truths / you had no milk / you fed me angels' meat instead / you had no blankets / you wrapped me in hair / you said i should never lie / taught me how to fight / said i should keep my wits about me / because anyone could turn against me / any time / any / one / even you / you taught me what i needed to survive / i hated you / i left you / i needed to / i think this / was your plan too

KITCHEN HYMNS

If anyone asks: 'How did Jesus raise the dead?'
kiss me on the lips, say: like this!

Jalal al-Din Rumi (translated by Fatemeh Keshavarz)

Kitchen Hymn

You showed up on the night of your birthday, you showoff.
Four months dead and you just amble in
with a grin and a raised eyebrow.

Hello my friend, you said. I opened my mouth to say
About time, but I wasn't sure what you knew.
I couldn't believe the ease of you. Outside, leaves fell.
The thrill I felt to share October birthdays.
This is the first autumn you'll not see.

You busied yourself with things:
making tea in my yellow pot,
Hey, I've got one of these, you said, and I said *I know*.
I bought it because I missed you, two days before you died.

You hummed, choosing cups,
that tune was always with you.
I watched you search my cupboards for a biscuit,
telling me about the books you'd been reading on the train.
Back turned towards me you said
Have you become a Protestant or something?
This place is far too tidy, and not a bite of chocolate in the house.

When I found that bottle of Paddy's that you gave me, I kissed and kept it.
Last week I sat at your desk and wept,
then went about my business:
an interview, a reading, a drive home through bright rain,

continuing the unfinishing conversation.
When you're quiet I fill the gaps. Like this.

The other day I saw something and reminded myself to remember what it was, so I could recall it when I needed it. I forget it now. What was it? A leaf? It's autumn, the green has gone to brass and berry, copper, ember, fire. Mulch underneath my feet. Was it the shape? Blades arranged around a centre? The way I could see how it would be part of something else's growth, eventually? There was a bird singing, I remember that, appealing for a mate, piercing the early air. I stopped because I'd stepped in hareshit and was wiping it away, there must be a form nearby. I know I was thinking about the night and how it grows, how the old story says that Eve worried the world was returning to nothing when the first winter of consciousness came. I was thinking of how I love the changing colours. I remember. I was feeling how good it feels to not have thought of you in weeks. The relief.

Jesus and Persephone Meet After Many Years

You look so much better, she said,
Older. Changed.
The scars are different too.

Thanks, he said.
Nothing would drag me back.

I just came up from Hades
yesterday, she said.

I figured you were coming, he said,
I waited for you all winter.
Then I saw buds on that old tree.
You look like you.

What do you do? she asked.

This and that, he said. But mostly
I walk the mountains, following the tracks
that animals make when they escape the hunt.

Hey, I always meant to ask you – is there more
than just one way?

Rite of Baptism

If you pass, know that you'll have no say
about what happens.

Some of our people will hate you.
You must create a life
without giving them all your life's attention.

Some people will delight in destroying you.
Some will strike you. Some will choose
others as their favourites.

Some have been waiting for you for generations,
circling, like hunters, round your little heart.
Of course they don't know you.

This truth will set you free,
eventually. But only after you've forgotten this.
You haven't learnt to fly yet, have you?

Someone will love you.
Someone will hurt you too, but you know that already.

We offer you little in the way of certainty;
just that the country you live in will not always be that country.

There is a lot you'll need to suffer.
Remember: help is a howl and an imperative. Nothing to be ashamed of.

One way or another, shame
can teach you what nothing else can teach you.

One way or another.

Your body is an event,
and you'll spend decades unpacking what's happened.

Here is what we cannot guarantee you:
guarantees, or history's purity.

Here is what we can: a stage, some paper,
curiosity, danger.

There is no such thing as the past.
Just stories of the past told today.

And anyway, nobody knows where the past begins –
in the beginning it was all a dream, not a story.

Remember: you must believe
some of this.

The Second Coming

there will be no fanfare
no trumpet no end of days

just the light on the leaves
of that tree you love to look at

no songs to sing
no one to beg

no resolutions no explanations
no solutions

no insight into time
no recrimination and no punishment

no guilt no reprimand
no judgement seat no mercy

just nothing darlings
nothing

[untitled/missæ]

I bless myself in the name
of the deer and ox,
the heron and the hare,
evangelists of land and wood
and air. The fox as well, that red
predator of chickens, prey of cars.
And the salmon and the trout
sleeping in the reeds.
When the wren wakes, I'll ask
her blessing, and if she comes out
she'll bring it. The squirrel buries
when she thinks no one else can
see. I bless myself in her secrecy.
There's a fieldmouse I've seen
scampering at dusk, picking up the seeds
dropped by the finches and the tits
throughout the day. Some nest of frenzy
waits her kindness and her pluck.
I go in the name of all of them,
their chaos and their industry,
their replacements, their population,
their forgettable ways, their untame natures,
their ignorance of why,
or how, or who.

Notes

Epigraphs:

Apostles' Creed translation is my punked-up version of the original.

Eavan Boland, 'The Pomegranate', *In a Time of Violence* (Carcanet, 1995)

Paul Celan, 'Psalm', *Selected Poems and Prose*, translated by John Felstiner (W. W. Norton, 2001)

'In the Name of the Bee' is the first line of an early poem of Emily Dickinson's.

Robert Graves, *The Greek Myths, Volume One* (The Folio Society, 1996)

Homer, *The Iliad* 8.16-20, translated by Emily Wilson (W. W. Norton, 2023)

Marie Howe, 'Magdalene – The Seven Devils', *Magdalene: Poems* (W. W. Norton, 2017)

Jalāl ad-Dīn Muhammad Rumi, 'Like This', translated by Fatemeh Keshavarz who recited it during an interview conducted by Krista Tippett, *On Being*, originally broadcast March 1, 2007

Patricia Smith, '34', *Blood Dazzler* (Coffee House Press, 2008)

The hymn 'Caoineadh na dTrí Mhuire' is collected in many places, including Donla uí Bhraonáin's *Paidreacha na Gaeilge / Prayers in Irish*, Cois Life Teo., 2008 (Translation my own.)

Paul Valéry, *Collected Works of Paul Valéry, Volume 14: Analects*, translated by Stuart Gilbert (Princeton University Press, 2016) although in this instance, the translation is my own.

Many of the titles from the sequence 'In a Garden by a Gate' are taken from scriptural texts, occasionally retranslated, punched or punked up by me with no permissions sought. Other poem titles take their name from the following publications: *Man's Search for Meaning* (Viktor E. Frankl); *Being and Time* (Martin Heidegger);

'The School of Dreams' (a chapter title in Hélène Cixous's *Three Steps on the Ladder of Writing*); *Desire and Its Interpretation* (Jacques Lacan).

The form and placing of the hellpsalms owe much to Leonard Cohen's magnificent *Book of Mercy*, originally published by Villard Books in 1984 and republished in 2019 by Canongate.

Acknowledgements

'Do You Believe in God?' [I don't believe in God, I said] is for Gail McConnell. 'Do You Believe in God?' [I accepted it for far too long] is for Raymond Antrobus.

The first drafts of this manuscript were written as the creative component of a PhD at the University of Glasgow under the expert and patient supervision of Heather Walton and Sam Tongue. Later, Cary Gibson supplied notes that only Cary Gibson could supply; Greg Fromholz showed love, support and curiosity all along; Pat Bennett held and beheld the emerging strangeness; Krista Tippett embodied and encouraged the phenomenology; Glenn Jordan, though he'd died, kept half an eye on me; Marie Howe steadied my gaze when everything disappeared; Martha Sprackland and Michael Wiegers are living reminders that 'editor' shares etymology with 'bring about'. Thanks to Clare Conville, Lizzie Milne and Anya Backlund for doing more than any three people could do. Thanks to Claretta Holsey. Thanks to all at CHEERIO Publishing, Copper Canyon Press, C&W Agency and Blue Flower Arts. Cover gladness goes to Keith and all at Mini Moderns; and to Phil Kovacevich for the hymnody.

Thank you to those who've given time, feedback, attention, protest and pressure to these poems, in direct conversations, or slant ones where I stole without your knowledge: Patience Agbabi, Raymond Antrobus, Ellen Bass, Fiona Benson, Sophie Cabot Black, Jericho Brown, Jamie Byng, Melanie Ciccone, Peter Coleman, Mark Conway, Paul Doran, Leah Doyle, Nick Flynn, Sean Foley, Vievee Francis, Chris Fry, Doug Gay, Stace Gill, Lorna Goodison, Phil Harrison, Joe Henry, Major Jackson, Zaffar Kunial, Dave Lav, Toby Martinez de las Rivas, Donna Masini, Jayne McConkey, Gail McConnell, Susan McNerlan, Vahagn Minasian, Joe Minchik, Marty Moran, my colleagues at *On Being*, Julie Perrin, Victoria Redel, Peter Saunders, Mia Spiro, Michael Symmons Roberts, Chris Wiman, Alex Wimberly.

Attention is a shape that time takes: mo bhuíochas, agus grá ó chroí, a chairde.